Learning about Sex

a series for

2

the Christian family

Where Do Babies Come From?

for ages **6** to **8** and parents

Ruth Hummel

Illustrated by Janice Skivington

CPH
SAINT LOUIS

Book 2 of the Learning about Sex Series

The titles in the series:
Book 1: Why Boys and Girls Are Different
Book 2: Where Do Babies Come From?
Book 3: How You Are Changing
Book 4: Sex and the New You
Book 5: Love, Sex, and God
Book 6: How to Talk Confidently with Your Child about Sex
Book 7: Human Sexuality: A Christian Perspective

Acknowledgments

We wish to thank the following for their special contributions to the Learning about Sex Series:
Frederick J. Hofmeister, M.D., FACOG, Wauwatosa, Wisconsin, served as medical adviser for the series. Micheal J. Chehval, M.D., urologist and chief of staff at St. John's Mercy Medical Center, St. Louis, Missouri, provided an additional medical review.

Rev. Ronald W. Brusius, secretary of family life education, Board for Parish Services of the LCMS, served as chief subject matter consultant.

Kathryn Krieger and Rodney Rathmann, Day-Midweek Department, CPH, contributed special expertise in the review and editing of manuscripts.

The following provided invaluable help in their areas of expertise: Darlene Armbruster, board member, National Lutheran Parent-Teacher League; Betty Brusius, executive director, National Lutheran Parent-Teacher League; Margaret Gaulke, elementary school guidance counselor; Priscilla Henkelman, early childhood specialist; Rev. Lee Hovel, youth specialist; Robert G. Miles, Lutheran Child and Family Service of Michigan; Margaret Noettl, family life specialist; and Bonnie Schlechte, lecturer on teen sexuality.

Editor's Foreword

This book is one of a series of six designed to help parents communicate Christian values to their children in the area of sexuality. A seventh book, *Human Sexuality: A Christian Perspective*, deals with the spiritual, emotional, and physical aspects of the God-given gift of sexuality. Both the single adult and the married will profit from the practical, biblically oriented content of this last book in the series.

Where Do Babies Come From? is the second book in the series. It is written especially for children ages six to eight and, of course, for the parents, teachers, and other concerned grown-ups who will read the book to the child. (See the "Note to Grown-ups" on the next page for suggestions on using the book and ways to communicate Christian values in sex education in the home.)

Like its predecessor, the new Learning about Sex series provides information about the social-psychological and physiological aspects of human sexuality. But more: it does so from a distinctively Christian point of view, in the context of our relationship to the God who created us and redeemed us in Jesus Christ.

The series presents sex as another good gift from God that is to be used responsibly.

Each book in the series is graded—in vocabulary and in the amount of information it provides. It answers the questions that persons at each age level typically ask.

Because children vary widely in their growth rates and interest levels, parents and other concerned adults will want to preview each book in the series, directing the child to the next graded book when he or she is ready for it.

In addition to reading the books, you can use them as starting points for casual conversation and when answering other questions a child might have.

This book can also be used as a mini-unit or as part of another course of study in a Christian school setting. (Correlated video and study resources are available for both curricular and home use.) Whenever the book is used in a class setting, it is important to let the parents know beforehand, since they have the prime responsibility for the sex education of their children.

While parents will appreciate the help of the school, they will want to know what is being taught. As the Christian home and the Christian school work together, Christian values in sex education can be more effectively strengthened.

Rev. Earl H. Gaulke, Ph.D., D.D.

A Note to Grown-ups

In story form, this book answers most of the questions about sexuality that six- to eight-year-olds typically ask—or wonder about. Most children this age will have difficulty reading the book on their own. So *do* plan to enjoy reading it *with* your child. Depending on her or his interest, read all of it at one time. Or read one chapter at a time.

Make it just another book that you enjoy reading to or with your child at those special times—just before bed? after homework? Once you've read it, of course, you may want to read it again and again—next month or even next year, when your child is at a different developmental level and able to absorb more of the content.

Take your time as you read, expanding on the text when your child asks for further information. Most of all, use the occasion to wonder at the beauty and design of God's good gift of sexuality. After all, what we're most interested in is building in our child a reverent, wholesome, responsible attitude about human conception and birth. We want to communicate not only truthful and accurate information about sexuality, but especially a deep appreciation of God's marvelous design and purpose. "God made me a boy (a girl)—and His creation is wonderful!"

Here are five easy-to-remember guidelines to keep in mind as you answer questions (each begins with a C):

1. *Commend* your child for asking and for coming to you, especially if the question makes you uneasy! You want to keep the channels of communication open.

2. *Clarify* the question: "When you ask, 'Where do babies come from?' do you mean, 'How do they grow?'"

3. *Connect* your answer to what your child already knows (or thinks he or she knows): "Remember what you learned about…? Well, that will help you understand that …" Also, you may want to connect your child's question to other aspects of growing up, thereby avoiding the danger of isolating sex from the wider background of life in general.

4. *Communicate* with simple, direct answers.

5. Let *Christ* Himself be in all that you say and all that you model about sexuality—He who "loved the church and gave Himself up for her to make her holy, cleansing her by the washing with water through the word" (Ephesians 5:25–26). So we can share with our child: "Isn't it *wonderful* that Jesus, God's own Son, was born as a baby! He grew up—just as we do. So He knows what it's like when we feel lonely or afraid. He always did what was right—and He died on a cross—to pay for our sins. Now we can be sure that God, our Father, forgives us. And we can be glad that Jesus is there to help us grow as God's loving child."

Suzanne Has a Birthday

Suzanne was seven years old today. She could hardly wait to get home from school.

Her daddy, her mom, and her grandpa were all waiting. Grandpa always came over when there was a birthday or something else special.

"You need me to help you celebrate, don't you?" he said with a wink. Suzanne agreed as she gave him a hug. Then she saw her birthday cake.

"O-o-oh, it's pretty!" she said. And it was! It had lots of yellow roses and seven blue candles. They were all burning while she opened her presents. There was a cooking set, a pair of in-line skates, and the game she had wished for.

"How did everyone know just what I wanted?" Suzanne wondered. "They must know me pretty well."

After Suzanne blew out the candles, her daddy picked her up and gave her a bear hug. Suzanne giggled when she got her breath.

"Look how big our girl is getting, Mother," Daddy said. "Do you still remember how she looked seven years ago today?"

"Seven years ago, Suzanne, you had just been born," Mother said. "You looked beautiful to me! Maybe you were just another red and wrinkled baby to some people! But to me, you were perfect! I wondered how your fingers and toes could be so tiny. I saw that you had your daddy's brown eyes. And I prayed, 'Thank You, God, for such a fine baby.' "

"Yep," said Dad. "We thought you were really something special. Loud, all right, but very special! We were so glad God gave you to us. And wow! Did you change our family!"

"I changed our family?" Suzanne was surprised. "How could I do that? I was just a baby."

"Just a baby?" Daddy laughed. "Before you came, Suzanne, there were just Mother and I to love each other. But after you came, we had another person to love. Soon you learned to love us, too. So then there was a lot more love in our family than ever before."

"You mean each new baby brings more love to a family?" Suzanne asked. When Mother nodded, Suzanne said, "Then every baby does change a family."

"That's right," Mother said. "And families are always changing. They change in different ways. A family grows larger whenever a baby is born or a child is adopted. And people in the family are always growing older, and the babies are always growing bigger."

"I know a family where the children are teenagers," Daddy said. "They've grown taller than their mother and father."

"They'll be grown up soon," Suzanne said. "When they move away, that will make their family smaller again."

"That's what happened to our family," Grandpa said. "Our children got married. Then Grandma and I were a small family again."

"Sometimes a family may have just a father or a mother. Or, a family can grow larger when grandparents come to live with them," Mother said.

"Why don't you come and live here with us, Grandpa?" Suzanne asked. "Then our family would grow again."

"Someday," Grandpa said, "maybe I will make this family grow bigger. Just like you did, Suzanne, when you were born. When I first saw you, I knew for sure you belonged in this family. That funny little pushed-up nose is your mother's, for sure."

"But, how did I get her nose, Grandpa?"

"Well, babies born into a family often look like someone else in their family. Of course, God doesn't copy when He makes a new person. He makes each of us special—like no one else in the world."

"But what about John, next door?" Suzanne said. "I wonder why he doesn't look like anyone in his family."

"That's because he was adopted into his family," Dad explained. "He was born to another mother. She loved him but couldn't take care of him. John's parents wanted someone just like him for their family, so they adopted him."

"What does that mean—*adopted* him?" Suzanne asked.

"Well, Suzanne, it means they decided to make him their own child. They love him as much as if he were born to them."

"That's a different kind of family," Suzanne said.

"Families are different in many ways," said Mother. "Some families have just a mother or a father. Some families have only one child. Some families have many children. But in some important ways we are all the same. We are all people

✤ living together,
✤ loving each other,
✤ celebrating good times together,
✤ helping each other through bad times,
✤ caring about what happens to each other."

"It was God who thought of putting us into families," Daddy said. "Wasn't it a good idea?"

"I'm glad God put me into this family," Suzanne said. "It's just right for me."

A Trip to the Museum

"Bill's ready, and I am, too. Can we go now?"

Suzanne was so excited! She was going to the museum with Mother and Daddy. It was a special treat. They had promised Suzanne that she could take her friend Bill along and stay as long as she wanted.

In the car her Daddy asked, "Well, Suzanne, what are we going to see first?"

"Oh, the baby chicks hatching!" Suzanne didn't have any trouble deciding that. "They are my favorite thing in the whole museum." And she told them all about the little, fuzzy yellow chickens sitting under the light to keep warm.

At last they were going up the steps of the museum. "Look, Mom, a balloon man! May I have that pretty blue one? Please?"

"Okay," said Mother as she paid for the balloon. "But don't I ever get to see those chickens?" Mother complained.

"Sure, they're right over this way."

"Oh, look," Suzanne whispered. One little chick was just pecking his eggshell. Suzanne was so excited she almost stopped breathing. Peck! Peck! They could all hear the tiny sounds from inside the egg. They watched quietly until the eggshell fell apart.

"Ooh, how wet and tired he looks!" Suzanne said. "Now he'll have to sit and rest until his feathers start to dry and get fluffy."

"I know babies don't hatch like chicks do," Suzanne said softly. "But I wonder just how they do get born anyway."

"H-m-m-m," Daddy said. "That's a big question."

"If you are finished watching the chickens," Mother said, "we may be able to find out over there by that blue sign."

"Oh, look! How tiny that baby is! I have never seen a baby that little."

"Hardly anyone does! When a baby is that tiny," Mother explained, "it can't eat or even breathe for itself. It has to live inside the mother's body. God made a special place for a baby to grow. It is called a *uterus*."

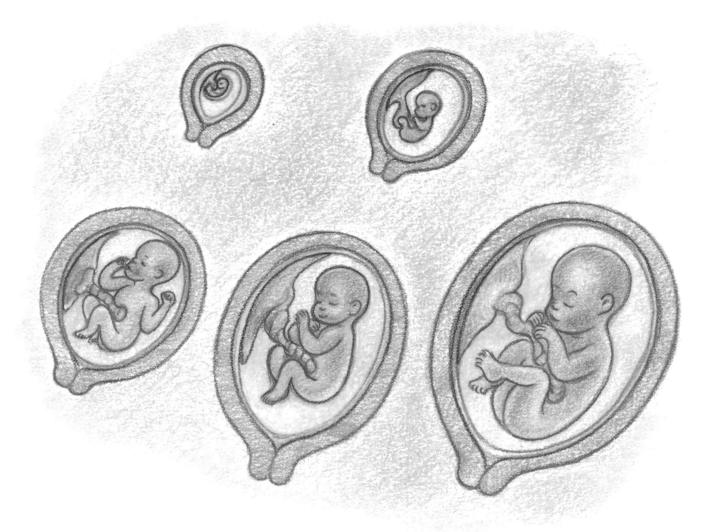

"A *you-ter-us*?" The word sounded strange, but it wasn't hard to say. "What is the uterus like? Is it a little room?"

"More like a little balloon," Mother said. "Look, I'll show you." She took Suzanne's balloon, let some air out until it was about the size of a pear, and said, "It's just about this size. And it's hollow inside, too."

"The tiny baby settles down near the side. The side of the uterus is much thicker than this balloon. That is where the baby grows."

"Here's a baby when it is bigger. Look!" Bill said. "See those cute little fingers and those tiny little toes! And look at that little mouth."

Suzanne wondered aloud, "Can a baby eat with such a little mouth?"

"No, it can't eat when it is so tiny," Mother explained. "It doesn't need to eat while it is in the mother's uterus.

The baby gets its food
from the mother's body.
See that cord going from the
baby's tummy to the side of
the uterus? Food from the
mother's body comes to the
baby's body through that cord
so the baby can keep growing.
The baby can't breathe yet,
either. So oxygen comes
through that tube, too."

"Was I ever that little, that
I couldn't breathe?" Suzanne
wondered.

"You sure were!" Daddy
said. "Even somebody as big as
me was that small once."

"It was a good thing you both
had a mother to be connected to,"
said Mother. "Do you know
where your cord joined your
body, Suzanne?"

"Right in the middle some-
where, I guess," Suzanne
answered with a little giggle.
"At my belly button?"

"That's right!" Daddy
chuckled. "Sounds like you were
buttoned onto your mother. The
real name for that place is *navel*."

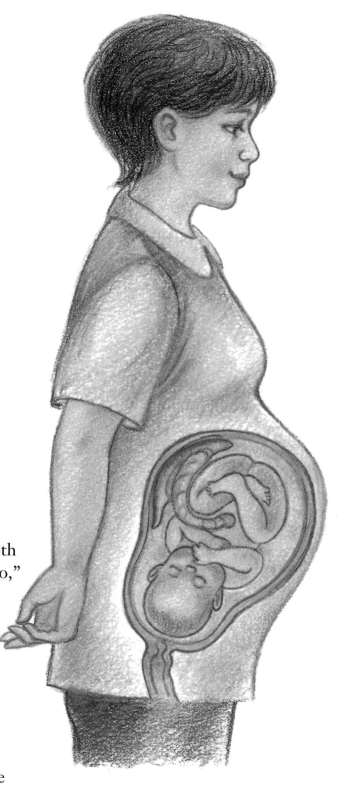

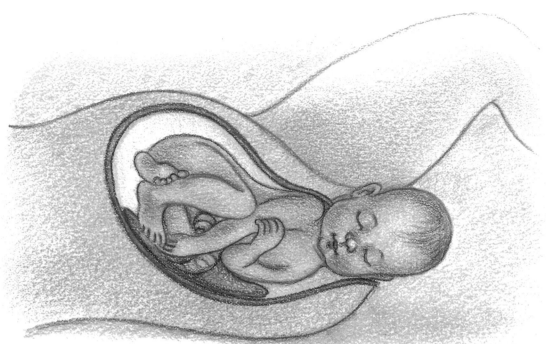

Another thing seemed strange to Suzanne. "I wonder why these babies don't have any clothes on," she said.

"They don't need clothes," Mother said. "It's warm and comfortable in the uterus."

"But how can they ever go to the bathroom?" Suzanne asked.

"Oh, they don't have to." Mother pointed to the cord again. "That cord takes care of everything. While the food goes to the baby's body, the waste goes from the baby's body to the mother's."

"Oh, I see," Suzanne said. "But it must get pretty crowded in there when the baby gets bigger."

Daddy laughed. "It is cozy, all right. Baby has to lie all curled up, with his legs bent and tucked under his chin."

"Look how big this next baby is!" Suzanne said. "Is there still enough room for such a big baby?"

"Bring me your balloon a minute," Daddy said. "What would happen to this balloon if you blew more air into it?"

"I guess it would get bigger," Suzanne said.

"That's the answer," said Daddy.

"You mean the uterus gets bigger like a balloon?"

"That's right, Suzanne," Mother said. "As the baby grows, there's always room for it. When the baby grows this big, the mother's body becomes big and round. Now everyone can see that the mother has a baby growing in her."

"You mean she gets fat like Grandpa?"

"No, no," Mother said. "It's not the same as being fat."

"We say she is *pregnant.* After the baby is born, the uterus will slowly go back to its normal size again, just like when air goes out of a balloon!"

"How does the baby get born then? Does the uterus break open like when a balloon gets popped?"

"Oh, no, Suzanne," Mother said. "The uterus has an opening something like a balloon has. That opening can stretch, too. When it is time for the baby to be born, it comes out through the opening."

"Is that how I was born?" Suzanne asked.

"Yes, Suzanne," Mother said. "That's how you and I and everyone in the whole world was born. That is God's way of bringing new people into the world."

"I don't understand it, but I think it's wonderful, don't you, Daddy?"

Daddy agreed. "That's why they call it 'the miracle of birth.' "

Boys and Girls—Fathers and Mothers

"Hey, Suzanne!" Someone was calling. Suzanne looked outside. Bill and his little brother, Freddie, were running through the rain to her porch.

"Can we play at your house?" they wanted to know.

"Sure," Suzanne said. "Come on in. What do you want to play?"

"Well, we can't play ball because it's raining," Bill said."Besides, I have to take care of Freddie. You know what four-year-old kids are like!"

"What can we play?" asked Freddie.

"I got a new cooking set for my birthday," Suzanne suggested. "Why don't we play house?"

"Oh, goody! I like to cook," said Freddie. He put a pot on the stove, found a spoon, and started stirring. "Can I be the mother?" he wanted to know.

Bill and Suzanne laughed. "You can't be the mother, Freddie," Suzanne said. "You're a boy! Only girls can be mothers."

"Boys can too be mothers, can't they, Bill?" Freddie thought boys would all agree on this.

"Well, I guess you can pretend to be a mother if you want to," Bill said. "But, really, only boys can be fathers when they grow up. And only girls can be mothers."

Freddie still wasn't sure. "I can be anything I want when I get big," he insisted. "Dad said I could!"

"Your dad meant that you could be an airplane pilot, or a firefighter, or even a cook," Suzanne explained.

"Yeah," Bill said. "He didn't mean you could be a mother. Only girls can be mothers."

"That's right," Suzanne chimed in. "God made girls with a special place where a baby can grow inside them," Suzanne patted her tummy.

"I wonder why it's in their stomach." Freddie looked puzzled. "With all the hot dogs and pancakes and ice cream?"

"Yeah!" Now Bill was wondering, too. "I forgot what we saw in the museum," he said. "Where *does* the baby grow?"

"It's not in the woman's stomach. It's in a special place called the uterus," Suzanne explained. "It's inside the body, so you can't see it."

"If you can't see it," Freddie said, "how do you know I don't have one, too?"

"Nope, Freddie," said Bill. "You can be sure you don't because you are a boy. Boys have their own special body. They grow up to be fathers."

"You mean all boys have to be fathers?" Freddie sounded disappointed. "Can't I be a cowboy when I am big?"

"Of course, Freddie," Bill laughed. "You can be a father and besides that almost anything else you want to be, even a cowboy."

"Oh, we're lucky," Freddie sang. "Boys can be more things than girls."

"Won't you ever get it straight, Freddie?" Suzanne was tired of explaining everything. "Girls can be just as many things as boys. I can be a mother and a lot of other things, too. I can be a teacher or even an animal doctor."

"Well, okay. Then I'll be the father," Freddie decided. "But I still want to be the cook, too. I'm going to make some hamburgers." And Freddie started banging around with his pots and pans again.

In Mother's Workroom

"Mother, where are you?" Suzanne called when she got in the house. She was hungry.

"I'm here in the workroom," Mother answered. "Why don't you get a cookie and come and visit a while?"

I wonder how she knew I wanted a cookie? Suzanne thought. Then she called, "May I have two, please?"

"Okay, Suzanne," Mother answered. "But put the lid back on the cookie jar." "M-m-m! These are good," Suzanne said when she got to the workroom. "Thanks a lot."

"You sure had fun with Freddie and Bill yesterday," Mother said as she arranged some silk flowers in three bunches.

"Uh-huh," Suzanne said and took another bite. "I like playing house. But Freddie sure says some funny things."

"Like what?" Mother asked as she got out her glue gun and began to attach the flowers to a wreath.

"Well," Suzanne said with her mouth still full of cookie, "he wondered why he couldn't be a mother. And I remember he even said babies are always messy, and crying."

"Well, they do cry a lot. But that is the only way they can tell someone they're hungry or hurt or cold," Mother said gently, as she added some nuts and berries to the wreath.

"You mean crying is like talking?" Suzanne was surprised at that.

Mother nodded. "If they could say, 'Mommy, I want my diaper changed,' they wouldn't have to cry, would they?"

"I guess not," Suzanne said. "Are babies a lot of trouble?" she wondered out loud.

Mother laughed as she put her glue gun down. "Babies do need care. But lots of people still want babies. Why, do you suppose?" She sat down at the table and took a roll of ribbon, snipped off a piece, and began to make a fancy bow.

"'Cause babies are cute. And it's fun to take them on walks in their stroller," Suzanne said. "I do that with Anne's baby sister. And she laughs so hard when Anne plays peekaboo with her. May I have this piece of ribbon?"

"Sure, you may have it,"
Mother said. "I'm glad I wanted
a baby a long time ago. Now I have my
seven-year-old Suzanne to keep me company.
What about you, Suzanne? Won't you be happy
when we have a new baby in our family?"

"But … but I like being the only kid in this
family." Suzanne wasn't sure they needed any more kids. She tried to
make a bow out of her ribbon. "I hope you'll still have time to play
with me after we get a new baby."

Mother pushed away the wreath she was working on and gave
Suzanne a big hug.

"I've told you many times how much I love you. You will always
be my girl, Suzanne. You don't ever have to be afraid that I won't
have time for you. I like to do things with you. And you are getting
so big now. You do so many things for yourself—like taking a bath
and hanging up your clothes. Why, you're big enough to help Daddy
and me take care of our new baby."

Suzanne still wasn't sure. She picked up two flowers from the floor and pinned them to her bow. She looked at her mother. "It's hard to believe a baby is growing in you right now. What do you think? Will the baby be a boy or a girl?"

"We don't know yet. But soon the doctor will do a test that will be able to tell us," Mother said. "But one thing we know now. It can *kick*."

"Is it kicking now?" Suzanne asked.

"Yes, Suzanne," Mother said. "Put your hand right here and you can feel the baby moving."

"Ooh, I can," Suzanne said. "The baby is really moving."

"Isn't that exciting!" Mother said as she gave Suzanne a little squeeze. Suzanne had lots to think about as Mother flipped the wreath over to fasten a hook on the back. "Will the baby have to sleep in my room? I don't think there would be room for another bed. Anne's baby sister has lots of other baby stuff, too."

"Oh, no," Mother held up the finished wreath to admire. "The baby will have this room! All my crafts will be moved to the basement. Would you like to see the new curtains I bought for the baby's room?"

Mother held up the curtains for Suzanne to see. "These curtains will be just right for a baby's room, don't you think so? We'll put them up when Daddy finishes painting the walls. He said you could pick out the color. What color do you think would look nice with these curtains?"

Suzanne thought yellow would, because there were little yellow ducks all over the curtains. Mother thought that was a good choice, too.

"I bet I know what the baby will sleep in—my baby crib!" Suzanne was starting to get a little excited about getting ready for a new baby. "Can we get my crib down from the attic?"

"Not so fast!" Mother slowed her down. "It will be quite a while before the baby gets here. It will be about four months yet. Time enough to finish this room. We'll have to buy some new baby clothes, too."

"Can I make something for the baby," asked Suzanne, "maybe a toy or a bib?" While she was thinking about what she would make, Mother got out the vacuum to clean up the rug. When the vacuum finally stopped, Suzanne got a chance to ask another question. "Did the baby start growing a long time ago?"

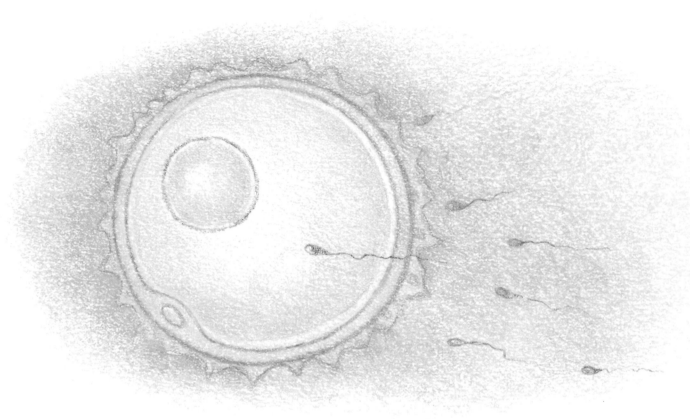

"Quite a while ago. It takes a baby nine months of growing till it is ready to be born. That's just as long as it took you to go through first grade."

"But what started the baby?" Suzanne wanted to know.

"That's another miracle. God planned it so that it takes both a mother and a father. You see, every baby begins when two tiny parts join together and start to grow. One of these parts comes from the mother's body. It is called the ovum. The part that comes from the father's body is called the sperm."

"You mean daddies help babies start?" Suzanne was getting another surprise.

"Of course," Mother pinched her cheek. "You are Daddy's girl, too, aren't you?"

Suzanne laughed, "That's what he says every time he swings me around and around. But how do daddies help babies start?"

"When a husband and wife love each other, they show it in many ways," Mother began.

"I know, they kiss each other and hug."

"That's right," said Mother. "They do things for each other, and they want to be together always."

"Is that when they get married, and they're a bride and groom and everything?" Suzanne put her ribbon on her head and pretended it was a veil.

"Yes, God is happy when two people decide to get married and start their life together with His blessing," Mother continued. "He made them for living together and showing their love to each other all their life. At special times they like to hold each other very close. God made their bodies so they fit together in a wonderful way.

"At those times the sperm from the man's body can go into the woman's body. Sometimes a sperm and an ovum join in the mother's body. That is when a new baby begins."

"And that's why a baby belongs to both his father and his mother!" Now Suzanne understood.

"Yes, that's the way God planned it! Both mother and father have a part in making the baby, but God has the biggest part!"

Daddy Is Home

"So this is where my family is!" Daddy was home. "Have you two been hiding on me?" He squeezed Suzanne's hand and bent over to kiss Mother. "Or should I say three?" he asked.

"Three?" Suzanne wondered why Daddy said that. Then he patted Mother where she was getting round in front. Suzanne said, "Oh, I know what you mean. We've been talking about the baby."

"Good! And what have you ordered? A boy or a girl?"

Suzanne had to think about that. "We don't know that yet. But we will know for sure when we see it."

"Oh, really?" Daddy laughed. "And how will you know then?"

"Because baby boys' bodies are like their daddies', aren't they? And girls' bodies are like their mommies'."

"That's right!" said Daddy. "Both boys and girls have the body parts they need to be fathers or mothers when they grow up."

"But what are those parts?" Suzanne wanted to know.

Mother answered, "When a baby girl is born, she already has the parts she'll need to be a mother. A girl's uterus, you know, is inside her body. Then she has a *vagina*. This connects the uterus with the outside. The baby comes out into the world through the vagina."

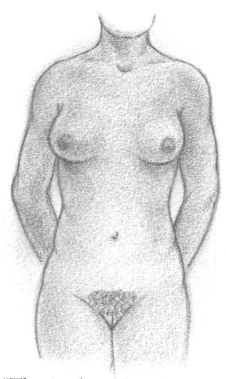

"But where is my vagina?" Suzanne wanted to know.

"It's the opening between the one for urine and the place for bowel movements," said Mother.

"Can I see it?" asked Suzanne.

"No," said Mother. "What you can see are the folds of skin, something like lips, that cover the opening of the vagina. This is called the *vulva*. These folds of skin can easily be seen."

"Well, on the boy's body," Daddy said, "the parts you can see are the penis and the scrotum. The part that looks a little like a finger is called the *penis*."

"That is where the urine comes out," Mother explained. "Also, when a boy becomes a man, at special times, sperm will pass out through the penis."

"The *scrotum* is the sac between the legs just behind the penis," Daddy continued. "The scrotum holds the *testicles*, which are pretty important."

"After a boy grows up, the testicles start making the sperm I told you about," Mother said.

"Boys and girls are really different," Suzanne said. "I wonder which is the most important."

"There are many ways in which boys and girls are the same," Mother reminded her. "They can both grow, think, feel, and love. It is interesting that God planned for just about the same number of boys and girls to be born. So both of them must be important to Him."

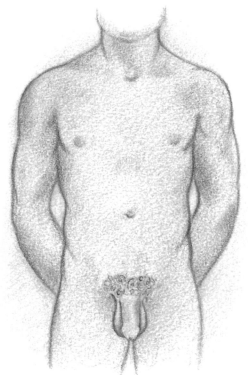

Loving and Caring for Each Other

"Suzanne," Mother called,
"will you please come and set the table for supper?
It's almost time to eat."

"Coming!" Suzanne followed the good smells into the kitchen.
As she put the knives and forks beside the plates on the table, a big
round pizza came steaming out of the oven. Umm-m, it smelled
delicious! Mother poured the milk and told Suzanne to call Daddy
to supper.

"I'm as hungry as a bear," he said as he sat down and put his
napkin on his lap.

"Me, too," Suzanne echoed.

When everyone was sitting down, they folded their hands to pray: "Come, Lord Jesus, be our Guest. Let these Your gifts to us be blessed. Amen."

"Is the new baby one of God's gifts to us?" Suzanne asked as soon as she had helped herself to a piece of pizza.

"The baby will be God's gift to all of us in this family," Daddy agreed. "We will all enjoy the baby. We can all help take care of it, too."

"Isn't it the mothers who take care of the babies?" Suzanne asked.

Daddy said, as he cut another piece of pizza for her, "Fathers and sisters and brothers can all help keep babies clean and comfortable and make them feel happy and loved."

"Did you help take care of me when I was a baby?" Suzanne asked as she took a big drink of milk.

"Did I ever!" Daddy remembered. "When you were little, you had tummy aches almost every night after supper. I used to put you on your tummy and lay you on my lap. I'd bounce you a little, then pat you a lot. That seemed to be the only thing that would make you stop crying."

Suzanne wanted to help take care of the baby, too. "Will I be able to hold the baby on my lap?"

"Sure you'll be able to hold the baby," Daddy promised, "as long as it doesn't wiggle too much."

"Will I be able to feed it, too?" Suzanne wondered.

"No, not at first," replied Mother. "Newborn babies need only milk, and I plan to nurse the new baby just as I did you."

"You mean you're going to be the nurse if the baby gets sick?"

"No, no!" laughed Mother, "I should have explained that word, *nurse*. When babies are born, their mothers have milk in their breasts to feed them. This is how God provides just the kind of food the baby needs. The baby snuggles close to Mother's breast and drinks the milk, and feels very much loved."

"Babies don't know very many things when they are born," said Daddy. "But no one has to teach them how to suck. They know that! They suck on fingers and pacifiers. They suck almost anything they can get into their mouths."

Suzanne laughed at that, then she remembered. "Anne's little sister drinks from a bottle with a nipple on it. I wonder why she gets her milk that way."

Mother knew about that, too. "Some mothers feed their babies milk from bottles. That milk helps them grow strong and healthy, too. Those mothers also love their babies very much. They hold them close, cuddle them, talk to them, and smile at them."

"You and I will be able to help feed the baby later, Suzanne," Daddy said. "When it is ready for cereal and fruit juice and baby food."

"But we can talk to it and play with it and love it, can't we?"

"We sure can," Daddy said as he picked her up. "And that's a very important part. That's what families are for—loving each other. It's all part of God's plan."